the original buckwheat

poems/reg E. gaines

*To Vilma + oops Vanessa
Hope You Like!
Paz + Love
R.E.g
2/2/99*

the original buckwheat
poems by reg E. gaines

edited by danny shot
cover art — *the original buckwheat* by kilolo
    kumanyika
cover art photographed by gordon gaines, sr.
front cover design by elizabeth van itallie
layout by michael cote

© 1998 by reg E. gaines
all rights reserved

library of congress catalog card number:
    97-076362

ISBN 0-9654738-1-3

some of these poems have been seen in:
aloud/bomb/long shot/tribes/wordup/
paterson literary review/ny times

"thanks to danny shot who never asked me to submit"

long shot productions
p.o. box 6238
hoboken, nj 07030

10 9 8 7 6 5 4 3 2 1

first edition

printed in the united states of america

the original buckwheat

poems by

reg E. gaines

long shot productions
hoboken, nj

— for my brother gordon

contents

poetical essays
christian haiku   8
d/klein   9
100 yrs/2 late   10
black/jack   11
thomas the burnt english muffin   13
maya...why ya write that poem   17
watermelons lox and bagels   19
off the wall   23
amos/andy and malcolm   26
jamaica to roslyn   30
just another mis/understood brother   34
for the lady in green   39
alzahn's song   42

violent urbanization
peace haiku   44
home alone   45
motherless child   49
blue/black plums   52
eulogy   55
when i grow up   59
how much more   62
pipe dreams   66
air jordans   69

bait   74
ta beat da heat   79
no good/goode   81
open season   83

margaret hague
urban haiku   88
blood on the keys   89
steppos attic   94
first time   96
149th & 3rd   99
por que tu padre   104
if she's darker than your sister   109
everybody   112
trane takes 5   114
chase/n e.k.   119
high page silence   121
welcome to mcdonalds   123
hoetry haiku   125

— poetical essays

christian haiku
if my name were christ
i'd definitely think twice
bout comin back here

d/klein

designer jeans sure look mean
but i wonder how long it took that
wide-hipped/big-ass sista
to stuff herself into jeans
made exclusively for women with that
very slim european look

seems like someone painted them shits
on her big/wide/behind
and she thinks she looks cute
real attractive

and in fact
she will attract
those whose minds are
full of lust
checkin out
her ass and bust

then she'll think
some niggas
sly/ass/wink
is a reason
for her to be flattered
but very soon
her morals will be shattered
but i guess they already are

cuz the minute she
pushed
and
shoved
and
squeezed
her big/black/ass
into them designer jeans
she had already gone
too far

100 yrs/2 late

blackman grinnin from ear to ear
feels no shame has no fear
blue/eyed woman at his side
does not know he lives a lie
got his whitegirl thinks she's fine
too good to be with his own kind
guess this brother just don't know
why blacks were lynched years ago
white women he could never touch
but now he can't get enough
of that "funky stuff"
thinks his whitegirl understands
and makes him feel like he's a man
this blackman's lucky perhaps it's fate
born 100 years 2 late

black/jack

i
wish i were black
what a thrill this would be
to see the world through the eyes of a
beat up
broke down
damn near dead
dark/e

i
wish i were black
what it must be like
to stroll with
infinite finger poppin rhythm
to be
rude
lewd
and crude color dark as nite

i wish i were black
in fact
when brother ray charles blows
a chill fills my ...
and i knows what he means
when he screams
"hit the road jack
and don't ya come black no more"

sure
wish i were black
to feast on
chittlins
grits
two-day-old fatback
smoke crack
get jacked by cops

who won't stop
beating me
and
beating me
and beating me
til
i'm/i'm/i'm/i'm
i'm a beat but
i ain't black
i'm...

lilac a lilly
silly as i wish
to be black
to be blue
to be bleached
to be blond
to be bricked
to be bombed
to be beat
to be broke
but hey jack
bein black
ain't no joke

so
goodnite
sleep tight
sweet dreamin
cuz jack
you got ta be black
without the beatin

thomas the burnt english muffin

you son of a
georgia sharecropper
the brand nubian showstopper
flip/floppin from left to right
afro-saxon fly by night
and we know
your wife's white

woulda coulda shoulda
been like thurgood
a
man who took a stand
but don't be mistaken
achin truth is
thomas
the burnt english muffin
wants to do his
bojangles shufflin
on the supreme court
but
homey don't play that
judge bork shit
so the muffins gonna have a fit
tryin ta git in

raised as a
new hope pope lover
mother theresa was his
holy rollin visa out a poverty
claimed he
pulled up his own bootstraps
perhaps
but ivory hands helped push

bush appointed him
so somethings wrong

all along claiming his
disapproval of quotas
not one iota
except when it fits his needs
leads one to believe
the burnt muffin
is least qualified
or are the presidents hands tie
george confide in me

has ct ever made a decision
check him out on colorvision
with his mouth wide open
gropin for words not there
so where is he comin from
sum total of the
disenfranchised american success story
raising old glory frantically
from sea to a shining sea of
red blood flowing knowing well
this racist system
condemns his people to hell

as he half smiles and replies
"no comment"
this satan sent
(disguised as a catholic)
triple pick six
does no good and much harm
as alarm clocks rock the boat
cuz we don't need
another judas goat
and a vote for you
who straddles the fence
makes no sense
as you rinse your hands of the
non-aborted bloodbath charade

parading down fifth
which you must take
baked in white ovens
burnt to a crisp
speak with forked lisp
mind confused
if your appointed
black people lose

and will thurgoods shoes
ever be filled
grilled cheese and tomato
on burnt english muffin
huffin and puffin
when it finally hits
"damn...
i ain't what i thought i was
cuz i
turns my back
and hears black nigger
and just can't figure it out"

no doubt you been brainwashed
your people squashed
hated/frustrated
while you've been checkmated
by george
and not the one from valley forge
but that

low/life ass wipe lizzard
who seriously considered
the former grand wizzard of the kkk
can you say
david duke of pearl white satin
and even if you don't speak pig latin
you'll understand his

oink/oink/boink/bam
the royal scam
another black pawn gone
as crosses burn on the whitehouse lawn
and supreme court justices sing along
to this free expression of
racial muck and mire

so thomas
you burnt english muffin
smell the smoke
wake the fuck up man
you're ass is on fire

maya...why ya write that poem

when the prez picked you
to pen that poem
i was thrilled to the bone
stone/cold/glad
slap jap nigga nappy
happy as a wannabee
stuck between
a rock
a river
a tree
yet it seems to me
you left someone out
hows bout the
cancellation of reservations
for hatians invitation
to this corrupt nations
inauguration
another manipulated manifestation
some come to know so well
just a game of show and
fell off
maya would you repeat part bout
rabbi and priest
explain why
few feast as nations starve
livin large layin low
oh say can you see the shining sea
let freedom ring
but maya i a thought you knew why a
caged birds sing songs of oppression
never confessin love for land
ruled by iron clad hands
standin in front of the whitemans
house negroe/house negroe/house negroe...
blowin poems bout melting pots
shots get hot

knotts burn
guess some never learn
correct manner
in which to burn
bimbette betsy's bullshit banner
filled to the brink with
wilted white rocks
bloody mary rivers
and true blue trees
but i knows the prez was pleased
with your vision of americas rebirth
cuz that razorback who jogs with hogs
thinks shit can't git no worse
wiley coyote
poormans j/f/k
hey maya
my maya my
ma/ma/ma/ma/ma/ma...
mammy
i's a thinks
you is kinda lost
cuz
what's so important bout you becoming
the second coming
of rhythmless robert frost

watermelon lox and bagels

wasn't the speech
on curriculum inclusion
that
caused confusion
labeled
race hating jew bating blind mans views
or the
anti-semitic satanic verse blues
front page news
media assasination
a quick combination of
libs to the left
dead wingers to the right
who
shed dim light on levins
quote
an anecdote of
how dumb blacks are
but only compared to whites
gunsites set
at jeffries head
for a two minute tirade
on
hollywoods gefilte fish parade
made in the shade
of systemic racism
a quick catechism
cuz those who got bank
can do what they want
like
flaunt their clout
scream and shout
then foam from the mouth
at the airport in wait
for jeffries to arrive

throwing knives at his back
"racist black nigger"
you figure it out
so much hate but wait
do words hurt
do words fight
whether wrong or right
they're just words
so
what did jeffries really mean
or is this merely
a hazey smoke screen
because the system
fails to lean
towards a multicultural education
their science fiction sensation of
distorted facts flying
from every side is
no longer viewed
as little white lies
they're soot and grime
muck and murk
the stuff which jerks
are weaned on
and this issues a pawn
to make us forget so
glue your ears
to the t.v. set
or get another dose
of the n.y. post/mortem polluted picture
and were
two minutes taken
out of context
and the next thing you know
is that cointel
disguised as the infamous
JDL

will assasinate jeffries
in the name of revenge when
they could have seen hollywood shuffle
and the muffled sounds of
"you fucking schwartzes"
"you cheap ass hebes"
leaves us obsessed
with messed up minds
working overtime
on the
who can hate who more debate
as crates of dill pickles
and pickled pigs feet
meet in grimey back alleys
and shining classrooms
looming larger than lucifer
spewing lies
hot as matzoh ball soup
smooth as sweet potato pies
and weeping children
wiping wet eyes wonder
why must blacks and jews fight
we need human rights
above all costs like
blacks brought from africa
to till the land
wait hand and foot
put in their place
or the haste with which (hate-off)
tried to wipe out a
people who suffered
a terrible fate
hate compounds hate
and is it too late
for us
to live in peace

so
cease and resist
unclinch the fist
wipe the hate from your heart
with clean bibs
because
blacks and jews can get along
we just need some
kosher spare ribs

off the wall

doin time
in the hundred watt soft-white sunshine
a.k.a.l.a.
layin way back
and forgot he was black
strange knack of knockin out hits
transforming pre/teens ta twits
pants don't fit and
gives me the jitters
cares more about his critters
than he does his own kind
as the
hundred watt soft-white sunshine
melts a mind so
dangerous
neither black nor white
boy or girl
this syncopated vanilla fudge swirl
twirls on toes
knows not who he is
loves liz
hates la toya
his only joy a
homemade zoo say boo
he's through the roof
aloof
not him
half-man in the mirror
admiring his million dollar grin
this mutant genius
without a penis
wants ta move to venus
so he can sex his play/toy bunny
but
maybe baby sis was

right on the money
cuz it sure ain't funny
when you get abused
losin all sense of identity
think m.j. might be confused
who he really is
wayout wacky wiz
dizzin in the emerald city
a modern day walter mitty
who can
be
all that he can be
except tan
yo
yous the man
makin all the rules
no 40 acres and a mule
for this starchild
as the cd's pile sky/high
critics lie
and say the shit sounds dope
nope...
then his sterile umbilical cord
ropes the competition
with this
nit/wit bullshit groin-grasping repetition
can he stand while pissin
kissin lips of chimps
this pre-vert pedophile
pimps kids
plays pattycakes with squids
then bids on the elephant mans remains
silly games yet
lifes no fun
needing to be # 1
in a crackless stupor
superstar shining bright
uses clorox at nite

believes his own hype
bloodtype
cold
bold as in bad
this honarary maytag tuff guy
with an ego the size
of the starship enterprise
lies/cries/dries fake tears
fears growing old
sold his soul to the
surgeon who's mergin his lips and his nose
so on with the show
cuz we know your
castrated
emasculated
insatiated
rape/dated
and hated by those who waited for
"the new songs"
ding/dongs at the gong show
checkin out king albino
hey mike gots ta go
but thought you should know
i remember the time
your face wasn't white
as snow

amos/andy and malcolm

well come on up my show is on
come on up its time
goodtimes i'm watchin goodtimes
yea
j.j. be crackin me up
makes me laff so hard my back be hurtin
man
you know what i like about him most
he looks like us
like a nigga spose ta look
big lips
big nose
big ass mouth
oh he funny
but you know what grandma say
always be mumblin bout what them two negroes
who use ta play amos & andy
would think of j.j. and martin and cosby
you know
the shit they do on t.v.
and i tell her
"grandma...
i don't care cuz the shit funny ta me"
but she just get all mad
start sayin how black folk
always talk about amos & andy
like they was two dumb niggas
but they was just doin what they had ta do
you know
ta make a way for us
for the future
she say they would be shamed
shamed if they seen what these fools is doin
dressin up like girls
grinnin them big old horse teeth grins
havin no respect for black women

cuz now you can call a woman a bitch on t.v.
and we ain't shamed but oughta be shamed
bout this music/this rap music
she say she oughta wrap that music up
thats right
wrap it up in some old newspaper
like they use ta do
when they finished cleanin them fish
wrap that shit up
and toss it in the trash
cuz it messin up these young folks mind
thats why they so disrespectful ta women
ta the elders
why the elders can't sit
thats right
sit on they own damn stoop
scared a gettin shot
and it be hot upstairs
and would be nice ta sit outside
and catch that motherfuckin breeze
but it ain't safe
and she say amos & andy
would be shamed if they seen t.v. today
and what would malcolm say
see
she love her some malcolm
didn't dig dr. king
cuz he always had his people singin
singin while they be gettin beat by them devils
but just mention malcolm
she go off
tell ya bout the time
she shook his hand right in front a 22 west
yea thats right
right down from harlem hospital
said he had this smile
and the nigga was fine
and i ain't never/did you hear me

never heard nobody call malcolm no nigga
but when grandma say it
it sound so right
thats right/thats right/that was her nigga
said he would be furious
would get a gun and start shootin
uh huh
shootin them triflin ass niggas
all up and down lenox avenue
said its a shame he ain't hear
cuz he would know what ta do
he would
cuz he been there
been on them drugs sellin drugs and women
was a thief been ta prison
was a dropout couldn't read
then he taught himself
so you can't blame schools
cuz you could do like malcolm and teach yourself
and all these young/boys busy dyin
while they mommas be blamin whitefolks
why they ain't like malcolm
follow malcolms lead
cuz you can read
can learn ta make your mind strong
and grandma get all caught up start cryin
everytime she talk about malcolm
everytime she think about malcolm
but me
shit
i like that malcolm jamal warner myself
thats right theo/on the cosby show
now he the kinda nigga goin places
and i bet that amos & andy
would be proud a theo
and proud a the cosby show too
cuz you know them two niggas
never dreamt bout no blackfolks

bein no doctors and no lawyers livin like that
but j.j. be makin me laff my ass off
and i could care less what grandma say
cuz i know malcolm laffin too
laffin at j.j. from his grave
cuz the niggas funny
and we got ta be funny
got ta make each other laff
cuz if we look at the world
the way the world really is
really is for blackfolk
we wouldn't be laffin
we'd be killin white people
so we need niggas like
j.j. and martin
and them wayans
and them townsends
cuz we ain't gonna get no more malcolms
we had our chance and he gone
and jesse
and farakhan
and west
and gates
and all them other fake malcolms
wouldn't take no bullet
no bullet for they people
like
malcolm did
like dr. king
did you see living single last week
latifah so funny
i know she do kinda act like a man
but thats why they call it actin
lordy/lordy/lordy
i sure loves me some t.v.

jamaica to roslyn

"next stop roslyn"
cried the grey balding man
collecting overpriced tickets
for the short uncomfortable ride

twenty women
speaking in dialects
strange but somehow familiar
traveling from places with names like
brownsville/bed stuy/harlem/the bronx/
but most have come from jamaica

they search for land of milk and honey
yet isn't it funny
how the wages they're paid
hardly make them able
to put milk
on their own dinner table

still...

their laughter
creates an atmospehere of joy
which envelopes the walls of the
dreary/steel/cab
whose destination is
da new south...

as they leave the train
bidding one another fond farewells
the range rover patrol
jockeys for position
with the
mercedes benz brigade
as the pungent aroma of
freshly baked onion bagels
fills the air

rear doors fling open
and the modern day slaves rush
to find their masters

salon tanned women
operating large dark sedans
where fudge-brown faces sit pompously
in plush leather seats
enjoying the view
and slowly chew
on
warm pieces of bread
while just up ahead
lies the estate
regal palaces of
queens and kings
marble gleaming
hot/tubs steaming
a silent somber peace
they've arrived in the land of
noveau riche

where
shiny satin tennis outfits
are the uniform of the day
and shrill voiced women
are proud
how little they pay the new slaves
who
cook/clean/iron/sew
and know
they're exploited
and do nothing
but grin and bear it
or be turned in to immigration
which will scare the shit out of you
if you're
hatian
jamaican

or just
black and poor...

so they fall to the floor
crusty knees
becoming more and more sore
scrubbing areas
large as tennis courts
which serenely sit
next to
elaborately constructed swimming pools
they thankfully
do not
have to clean

and though the work is hard
you can always hear the faint hum
of a bob marley tune
amidst the rancid odor
of scolding water and ammonia
rising from plastic buckets
into broad brown nostrils
causing silent tears to flow

but for the modern day slave
no one grieves
as cool spring air
rustles through money colored leaves
which sprout
from what seems like
a million trees
surrounding the estate
and i wonder if the new slaves hate
their masters

and their work is done
as the setting sun
signals the end of another day

"hey
here's your pay
hurry
don't delay
i've got to get you
to the station
right away
or i'll miss my appointment
with the plastic surgeon..."

as they climb aboard the
drab/metal cab smiling
deep/inside
they cry
and
false tales of
preferential treatment
swirl through the cab
like day old trash
in a
violent winter wind
as the grey balding man
cries out to this sea of
dark/wretched souls
"next stop jamaica..."

just another mis/understood brother

labeled psychedelic
though we called it noise
you could never be one of the boys
playin that
granite shit
too black 2 be white
too white 2 be black
yet
clapton/townsend/mc/cartney
and
big-lip mick
long ta suck your dick
cuz
you was the man
gave us all tickets ta ladyland
yet we refused ta go
didn't know bout axis
weren't experienced
nappy heads hard as the rock
you slingshot through our ears
but we didn't hear
so you left
stratocaster in hand
to this strange grey land of
cockney/royalty/l/s/d
soon ta be a legend
you had no friends
just parasites
flyin high as kites
pluckin/suckin/duckin fame
comin off as a
lame motherfucka
while we torched
our altered states
hatin you
for kissin frostys behind

we was ray charles blind
ta where you was comin from
never checked out
third stone from the sun
or machine gun
til you was dead
took one look at your
whiteboy styled
head of hair
knew you was no where
didn't care you were a part of us
resented the fuss
honkeys made over you
some nigga from seattle
who couldn't even play
and today
damn near thirty years later
princes hair
is even straighter than yours
heapin praise on the doors
like they was the shit
yet they've all stolen your
hits your clothes
the wild shows
proof
you can teach new dogs
old tricks
but you payed your dues
playin blues
on the chittlin circuit
takin shit
cuz you wanted ta jam
told ta scram by
threatened veterans
who saw those liquid brown fingers
on your magic left hand
command that strat ta
speak at will

cry/moan/shriek/shrill
you was bad
miles knew
lil richard did too
but most of us had no clue
it was like
fallin asleep
watchin the late show
and even black radio
wouldn't bring your noise
refused to excuse you while you
kissed the sky
said it was your
tie-dyed hair fried wind cried mary
thought you was a fairy but
you was just shy
all the while worryin
what we thought
you sought our support
yet few of us bought
your music
failed to help you through those
wild times
hard as the symbol
you'd now become
not drum but phallic
a quick-prick fix
to a dying industry
dominated by young white boys
who stole old blackmens songs
couldn't play
couldn't sing
then along the watchtower
came the wild thing
confused
abused
and destined to lose
but you saw the light the

first ray
tried ta break away
from that
acid rock back ta bee-bop
band a gypsys
you'd set us free
and with a single song
screamed to america
how wrong the war was
and your
blue/black abstract
givin patriotic americans
a heart/attack manner
in which you played the
star spangled banner
shook the world
while we concerned ourselves
with the skin color
of the girls you dated
frustrated peabrains
who failed to realize
the train you took
traveled at the speed of sound
yet we knew every verse of
hound/dog by elvis
shaking his pelvis
better than we knew your songs
except purple haze
a simple phrase
barless cage from which
you'd never escape
repeatedly raped
by fakes and snakes
taken advantage of
you were merely looking for love
and when you needed us most
we weren't there
scared ta claim you

as our own
now your
stone free/history
jimmy
we done you wrong
waited until you was long gone
before we listened to the
songs you played
emotions displayed like
depression
pain
and sorrow
but you pegged us all square
when you said
think i'd better wait til tomorrow

for the lady in green
(who shits in the harbor)

as a 60's like sunshine
streams through dim blinds
i slowly rise
my black-eyed mind
attempts to diguise
filth/degradation
in this nation of millions
which holds me back

precariously i crack
the crack sheet plastic window
to see some
snot/nose green
bimbo in limbo
standin tall
lookin proud
talkin loud
but sayin nothin

huffin and puffin her
roughly rusted tin chest
claims of best
foam from lying lead lips
hard nipples cripple
cancer infested breast
which tests my will
i should kill that whore
who shits at the door
of her tired her poor
her supposedly free
this piss stained pained
miss liberty

green stamp tramps
cold lampin foot camps
an my rope burned neck
cheap paint taints bitch
who ain't pc correct
microphone check one/two
one/two

limp dick swingin bringin
memories of poplar trees
and eli's gin
begin again
because he was not a
friend but a fiend as mean
as this mucous green gargoyle
laffin while we toil
in dirty water boilin at
a hundred and two
red white and
blue/balled monty halled
deals like meals on wheels
so get the fuck back in line

behind door #3
you win a free
trip to the tip of the
slip of your tounge
gun runnin funnin sunnin
confusin abusin defeat
take your war torn receipt
for bills shill bill of rights
forever over due
and you knew that i knew
that your time was through
bitch your through
witch your through
puta tu eres

your through
your time is up
so fucking corrupt
yea
its up
its up
uh huh
yup
your through

alzahn's song

only thing i give a fuck about
is lookin fly
why
you know
cuz my self esteem is low
ain't nowhere ta go but down
so when my feet hit the ground
gots ta have some new shit

— violent urbanization

peace haiku

motherfuck the beef
cuz if you ain't talkin piece
you ain't sayin shit

home alone

this hallways real cold
smells like piss
and it's dark
but i'm better off here
than some bench
in the park
my dinner consists of
crack/twinkies and chips
but it stings when i chew
through this
fat busted lip

a big burnt building
is where i call home
but i
really don't mind
always sleepin alone
its never much fun
but i only get sad
remembering times
my dad
got mad at
me
my moms
but i forget why
he'd slap her
then stomp me
and make us both cry
one nite i yelled
"yo!
you bloodided moms nose"
he screamed
"boy...
take off your
god/damn clothes

pops snatched the cord
from a
cheap plastic lamp
as my eyes became misty
palms sweaty
and damp
he swung like a madman
at my arms
and my head
the look in his eye said
he wished i was
dead

dashed to the
bathroom
locked the old door
stared
in the mirror
was shocked when i saw
blue/black bruises
cherry welts on my face
knew it was time
to cut out
of this place

dad was dead drunk
sprawled out
in a chair
was my time to
breakout
just didn't know where
slipped on button flys
high tops
a hood
three strikes i was out man
splittin for good
kissed moms
who was sleeping

beat up real bad
the longer i looked
the more i got mad
spied my pops wallet
dug
knee-deep inside
and
wouldn't you know it
he once again
lied

told moms he'd no dough
so we couldn't eat
yet smack-dab in my palm
thick/green and neat
lay
two hundred dollars
which i took as i fled
moment he sobered
just knew
i was dead

11 p.m.
scared out a my mind
what could i do
ta past this dark time
well a
dude on the corner
slid a vial in my hand
labeled
one-way ticket ta disneyland

stuff looked ta me like
pieces a soap
he said
"nah lil man
it's your bottle a hope"
he slid me a pipe

i slid em a ten
wouldn't be long
for i'd see him again

when thinkin about it
the shit seems real mean
but
i guess nowadays
you're grown up
at thirteen
but who can i turn to
or
who can i blame
for all of this madness
and all a my pain

as i
sit in my penthouse
and
gaze into space
eyes glazed in a daze
chasin a taste
i'm coolin
i'm groovin
gots no need to gripe
i just
flicks my bic
and
lites the damn pipe

motherless child

metal stroller
rolling manger
anger boils
ever rising
catching eye
of storm
of wave
as
new-age slave
pounds pavement with
papoose...

babe belongs
to another
absent mother
busy matching
mixing
mingling
diamonds dangling
while her offspring
learns to sing songs
from an island...

neon nanny
never smilin
blue/blood mommy
checking styles in
barneys
bon witt
lizard boots fit
tyke tastes tit
of surrogate
licks up every bit...

bids farewell
most everyday

not to work
but off to play
would not have it
any other
way away
while far away
not far away...

neon nanny's children stay
with their other
older mother
lessons learned
run for cover
bullets bounce off
project walls
scattered brains and
free for alls...

tiny tyke
crawls on fours
plush beige carpet
marble floors
mommy dearest
dips at shore
neon wonders
what's in store
for her poor
children...

then that day
that fateful day
took the tiny tyke to play
wandered cross
a bustling street
massive traffic
could not beat
pool of blood
twitching feet

mommy dearest
where were you
sailing on
the ocean blue
oh how could you
dare to
should you
label neon nanny nigger
figured it would
end this way...

grey sighs
lime green envy
glows when nanny
bring she babies
mommy dearest
stands the nearest
finally she
sees the clear/
rest in peace
child
rest in peace...

blue/black plums

it was hot
i think the hottest day that summer
there were so many of us out there
cuz not a single one of us
had no air condition
everybody was hangin on they stoops
or sittin drinkin cold beer on they fire escape
and it was sure hot but not that hot
cuz i told them fools not to throw her in
cuz when her hair got wet
it got nappy i mean nappy
and i never understood why her momma
called it a kitchen
said she had a kitchen on the back of her neck
now it was nappy
no comb nappy
but kitchen
i ain't know bout no kitchen
but butch and them
they wouldn't do that to the redbones
called em redbones which meant high yellow
if you was yella
butch and them would think you was fine
they must a been retarded or somethin
cuz some of the most ugliest girls
was high yella
lookin all sickly and pale
with them nasty red dots on they face
bitches walkin round
like they shit was beige
wasn't pretty
least not ta me
butch and them never throw no redbones
underneath the hydrant
just black girls
blue/black girls

girls be the color of them black ass plums
grandma mcduff always had on her kitchen table
they tasted sweet
and i always thought how sweet
when i seen some girl black like them plums
but i guess butch and them
ain't never taste them plums
cuz they grabbed her and she was screamin
and big and strong as she was
she couldn't stop them
cuz it was six a them and one a her
and everybody was drinkin and laffin
and it was hot
i remember it was hot/so hot
as they pushed her near the hydrant
she slipped
i seen it
heard her scream when she slipped
it was red
but not like cherries
like cheap muscatel everybody was sippin
kinda wine ain't never seen no grape
looked like that wine mixed in water
that filthy water from the hydrant
but what i remember most was the sound
sound of her head hittin that hydrant
then the sirens/loud ass sirens
and i was relieved
cuz least the ambulance was comin
and that was strange
cuz the ambulance hardly come here
i looked up from the blood
it was the cops
nasty ass cop with them rotten green teeth
green like leaves
and he ain't pay that plum no mind
busy yellin bout keepin the hydrant off
slappin butch and the other boys upside they head

and she lay still
and it got quiet
and it was hot
and i wondered
where was her momma
she was still layin still
like she was sleep
and the ambulance never came
and i never saw her again
but i still eat plums
but just the blue/black ones
and they makes me thinks of kitchens
makes me think of why
when i see these plums
these blue/black plums
i always starts ta cry
and its hot
its awful hot today...

eulogy

in this
tiny texas town
where lady justice
sports a
toilet tissue blindfold
to hide her
fabricated frown
some very strange shit
went down

carnation milk capital
of the
u/s/a
home to
annie ray dixon
is fixin to explode
you see
she was pricked
by a thorn
eighty-four
wired/worn/weary
teary-eyed
as cries ask
"why!"
did annie ray
have to die

shot by one
hired to protect
who neglected to
check it out
cuz when in doubt
men in blue conspire

liar claimed
at 2 a.m.

him and his boys
the tyler texas toy cops
never stopped
to contemplate
they just
lay in wait
behind an oakwood door
where
poor annie ray
sick in bed
all day long
battling pneumonia
when a

frank baggot
maggot brain
came a callin
and fallin
fire/n his piece
now annie ray
ceases to exist
but why didn't
maggot brain accidently miss
as the
twisted story
goes like this

officers/afraid
embarking on a
drug raid
made a mistake
some
scumbag informant
sent an
un/hip slip
of the
tounge type tip
telling tales

of cocaine sales
taking place at
annie rays crib
did a
keystone cops adlib
and busted in
but no drugs were found
sound familiar

annie ray
was made to pay
for anothers miscue
they blew her away
as she
meekly lay in bed
cold dead
and it don't even
matter why
cuz now this
killer cop
needs an alibi
claimed he cried
threw up his guts
yet it seems so corrupt
when he's given
temporary paid vacation

as our
midnite nation
screams
for human rights
p.o's and c.o's
point gunsights
at black targets
alabaster fingers
wet with sweat
itchin
twitchin

ready to pull triggers
on niggers
like
yvonne smallwood
eleanor bumpers
mary mitchell
annie ray
and how many more
each and everyday
must die
as we
bow our heads
and bid annie ray dixon
a sorrowful
good/bye

when i grow up
(i want to be just like john gotti)

manuel maji
spray painting graffitti
on corona queens wall
after dark
down the block from
spaghetti park

bludgeoned
despite being warned
to stay out of this
pizza slingin
saturday night fever swinging
neighborhood
inhabited by that
18 karat gold
crucifix wearing
brotherhood
forever willing to
fight and die
protecting their
pepperoni with extra cheese slice
of the american pie

"they ain't have ta kill the boy"
cried and angry resident
of this
olive oil place
"just smash his knuckles
crack some bones
break his face!
or use a stun gun
make that mooley run away
make him pay
for destroying our property"
and this sounds like a scene
from godfather III

59

"batter up
its louisville slugger time
spic tagged us
now lets tag him
his futures dim anyhow
pow!
did you see that fuckin blood
squirtin everywhwere?"
and this shit
scares the hell
out of me

god/damn
garlic breath breathin
grease-ball heathen
vigilantes
taking the law
into their own hands
clip-tounge speaking
nigger seeking
a 1990's version
of the ku klux klan
and another young man
is dead

and i'm fed up with these
guinea pigs
who don't digs
people of color like
manuel maji
who now
freely roams the heavens
while those
trans am driving gumbas
play video games
at their
local 7/11
but perhaps someday

we'll see a
cotton covered cloud
graffittied with black paint
which reads
"fuck you muscle/head guidos"
signed
manuel maji
spray-painting
graffitti saint

how much more
(can a loaf of challah cost?)

blacks and jews who
choose to snooze
lose their sense of identity
and the rebbi hates jesse
and jesse ate shit
bit more than he could
jew/baked black/jack
the card game a gamble
while honest abe stinkins
rambles bout freein
me and josh and
"oh my gosh
i just realized
neither of us eats swine"
so why the primetime hysteria
concocted by
mass media
the more the merry
a manipulation
in this
ignominous mini-nation
where kings are crowned
by the
dead of their living nites
so low on totem poles
terrified of
heights/lites
human rights
hasidic critics
who throw k.o. blows
like bo
you know
riddick
chump from crooklyn
whoops thats brooklyn

r/u hip
ta what i'm
trying to say
as eastern parkway
becomes the new
bay of pigs
bent twigs and fig leaves
in a borough labeled
little tel aviv
heave calm bombs
into unsuspecting ears
as tears flow slowly
through a
blood red sea
and community means

one is the loneliest number
you could ever
do unto others
before they smother your
ask me a question
i'll tell you no
lying on a
cold concrete slab are
arabs and blacks
sneak attacked partners
in death
rejected requests of
young and old
lives sold to the
n.y. times
screaming deadlines from
hate inflated egos
who know
best to boost
soupy sales tells truer tales
as we fail to assail the
sly the slick the wicked the

evil knievel can
jump the grand canyon
yet we can't abandon
randomn acts of violence
like pontious pilot rinsing
hearts/hands/minds
killing time
"die"
killing time to
"die nigga"
killing time to occupy
"die nigga die
fly high love dove"
scrub-a-dud-dub
two nations in a tub
will you rub my
black against jew
and you knew you was
right means white like
killin then chillin cuz
steel grey bars you never see
repeat after me
we
are the chosen ones
sons of the sun
not daughters of slaughter
serving up orders of
double-dish gefilte fish
too bad you missed my
black-eye peas
plopped on top of
uncle bens rice
and it must be nice
to have
"jew/mima"
play maid in the slave
as lubes toss
linguistic grenades
we battle a.i.d.s.

afraid our
dwindling african tribe
is forever lost
and how much more can a loaf of challah cost
frosty the snowman
damn sure cold
old as religion based on
pigeon turd
and the word of a profit
young gifted and black
step back
sneak a peek
see the meek
inherit the earth
and for what its worth
this ain't your land
understand why you
fight for rights
in this crown called heights
many nites of unrest
but the best will prevail
all hail
allah/jehovah/judah/budah/
bits of blood which drip
from the criss-cross colors
of a crucified christ
while the heist of ground
by the
lost/found
fake/brown
thorn/crown
cryptic cheesedick
savior of souls
moles in this hole
on this hell called earth
chosen/no/cursed
and whats worse
failure to acknowledge
that we were here first

pipe dreams

as i place my lips
on the scorching glass
and suck with all my might
i see maggot colored clouds
billow then bounce
which sends my mind racing upwards
higher
higher
higher
and higher

i feel the suns warmth
see the stars shine
rise above the atmosphere
head rushing
mind spinning
eyes squinting from
brightness of light
which is not really there
i feel powerful
invincible
i feel my feet
lifting off the ground
as i rapidly ascend
to heaven's pearl colored gates

suddenly
as quickly as i rise
my descent begins
a multitude
of fluorescent lights flicker
as i fall
non-stop
to the cold ground below

a deep depression
sweeps through my mind
as if it were
a brisk autumn wind
beckoning winter
and i fall
lights dim
it is darker

but i long to rise
to see again
the brightness
for i am crashing towards earth
towards reality
i so want to escape

and i fall
faster
i cannot breathe
faster
faster
i cannot
breathe
faster i
cannot
breathe breathe
faster
breathe i cannot
cannot faster breathe
faster i faster
cannot breathe
i...

and darkness
turns to blackness
as i
plummet downward
furiously fighting

desperately depressing
moods
which fill my
blackened soul
i cannot...breathe

my thoughts turn ugly
i hate
i hate
i hate my/self
so much
i would do anything
to leave this earth
like

suck the smoke
from this pipe of death
as i
fall and fall and fall
and then
the ground opens
and i'm
falling
crying
screaming
dying
am i
dreaming...

as darkness
becomes blackness
a deep deep sleep
what the fuck
i need the rest...

air/jordans

my air jordans cost
a hundred with tax
my suede starters jacket
says raiders on the back
i'm stylin/smilin
lookin real mean
cuz it
ain't bout bein heard
just bein seen

my leather adidas
baseball cap
matches my fake
gucci backpack
ain't nobody out there
looks good as me
but the shit cost money
it sure
ain't free

and i
gots no job
no money at all
but its easy ta steal that shit
from the mall
parents say i shouldn't
but i knows i should
gots ta
do what i can
ta make sure
i looks good

and the reason i have ta
look real fly
well ta tell ya the truth

man
i don't know why
guess it makes me
feel special in side
when i'm wearin
fresh gear
i
don't have ta hide

but i really must get some
new gear soon
or my ego will pop
like a ten cent balloon
but securities tight
at all a the shops
everyday there are
more and more cops

my crewz
laffin at me
cuz i'm
wearin old gear
schools almost over
summer is near and i'm
sportin torn jordans
and needs somethin new
only one thing
left ta do

cut school friday
catch the subway downtown
check out my victims
hangin around
maybe
i'll get lucky
and find easy prey
gots ta
get some new gear

theres
no other way

i'm ready
and willin
i'm
packin my gun
this is serious business
shit ain't no fun
but i
can't have my posse
laffin at me
cop somethin dope
just wait
you'll see

come out a the station
w 4th/near the park
brothers shootin hoops
and
someone remarks
"hey homes...
where you get them def nikes!"
as i says ta myself
i likes em
i likes

they was
q-tip white bright
and blinded my eyes
the red emblem
of michael
looked as if it
could fly
not one spot a dirt
the airs was
brand new
had my pistol
knew just what ta do

followed him very
closely behind
waited
until it was
just the right time
made a left turn on houston
pulled out my gun
and said
"gimme dem jordans"
nigga tried ta run

took off fast
didn't get far
i fired
fool fell
between two parked cars
he was
coughin/cryin
blood dripped on the street
and i
snatched them air jordans
off dat niggas feet

while layin there dyin
all the punk/ass could say
was
"please man (cough)
don't take my jordans away"
you think he be worried
bout stayin alive
as i took of with the jordans
there was
tears in his eyes

very next day
i
bopped into school
with my

brand new air jordans
man
was i cool
i killed ta get them
but hey
i don't care
cuz now
i needs a new
jacket
ta wear

bait

and
she passed by
tight black mini
ridin high
pretty yellow thighs
plump/juicy/jello behind
rockin back and forth
of course my dick got
hard as the lard
grandma used
when fryin chicken
bitch looked
finger lickin good
ta me
knew i'd soon be
fuckin her brains out
no doubt
in my mind
at all
titties big as
bowlin balls
pushin out from her
slinky dress
hair a mess
you know that
just got out a bed style
legs a mile long
couldn't wait
ta stick my ding/dong
in between her
golden arches
different
from mickey dees
cuz she looked like she
already served
a billion for free

so
why not me
i said
"baby...
you so fine"
but she wouldn't give me
the time of day
gots no play
while her dress
was sayin yes
even though
she might a meant no
so

i'm houndin
soundin like a
dog in heat
man
fuck all that talkin sweet
cuz if she
wanted me ta
buy her a rose
she wouldn't a
stuffed her ass
into them hoes clothes
and if
bo knows baseball
i know when a bitch
needs ta be
sprawled on the floor
beggin for more

followed her
to the
dark parking lot
knew she was
hot ta trot
soon a key would

fit the lock of her
samurai jeep
grabbed her from behind
threw her down on the front seat
and said
"keep quiet"
hit her in the face
tore that sleazy dress
tryin ta find a place
ta shoot my
loaded gun
young/dumb and full a come
her slurred words cryin
"no!"
as my jimmy
began ta grow larger
harder
rubbin her butt
smashed her head against the dashboard
and yelled
"shut/up slut!"
but my
lip was cut
bleedin bad
i was madder than mad
out a control
ravaging that bitches
sacred watering hole
tryin ta pound her ass
through the jeeps door
sweatin/foamin
givin it to her
like she
never had it before
shot my goo
and was through

zipped up
feelin no shame

cuz that
tramp was ta blame
wearin shit
that a make any hoe proud
those loud talkin
street walkin
bitch/bum scumbag fag/hags
who wags their tails
like dogs in heat
when in reality
ain't nothin but
pieces of meat
in my butcher shop
and the shit won't stop
til crazy motherfuckas
like me
are off the street
cuz i can do
anything i want
any time they
flaunt their wares
cares only bout them
see through blouses
mini skirts
fuck harmless flirts
which leads to
pain/stains
men insane
who've done this shit
since time began
you'd better understand
the shits on you
like one flew
over the cuckoos nest
crazy half dressed
big ass breast
another fuckin conquest
respect yourself

protect yourself
cuz where i'm from
woman are bait
which most men hate
deep inside
don't hide
shit ain't news
caught with your panties
down round your shoes
cryin the blues
bout bein
violently abused
by men
who truly believe
its the
right thing ta do
give them
ever quick
ta flick their bic
sadistic motherfuckas a chance
and they'll
do that shit ta you

to beat the heat

foamy frost
frozen jet spray
boiling hot
gots ta play
rainbow arc
dudes dark
configurate and wait
for man

b/boyz grandstand
hangin ten on
urban surf
2 tuff a turf
ta play lifeguard
hardened sand
tar/baby black
snackin on
oreos
laffin at
hammertoes
hoes/housewives
commonlaw
ripped from lip of
poormans shore

quick cure for
beatin heat
sweet mochas
high yellas
flirtin with fellows fried
sunburnt brown

underdrowned
purple/plum suede
snatched out shade
tossed in fray

silver spray sprouts
suede shouts out bout
knip-knaps knippin
at edge of kitchen
ass switchin
bitchin/bemoanin
tone/loc'd tonin
mind misplaced

chased by
new-wave slaves
slips/slides
on slickened surf
smittened/smurffed
cracks head on
blood lead pipe
waits for days
fights for life
blond bozo
once/twice
twists cap
slaps surfers back
unkindly reminds
to not touch hydrant
again

no good/goode

stupid ass niggas with guns
got more guns in the black community
than they got in some third world countries
but you ain't organized
got ta be organized ta get shit done
not like that dumb ass tellin them niggas
he'll give them toys for they guns
tradin in weapons for teddy bears
so what you gonna do when the enemy come
tuck em in and tell em a bedtime story
miltias sproutin like weeds in watts
and we got some fool tradin toys for guns
when every white person in america
got a god/damn bazooka in they basement
and he tradin toys for guns
but niggas better be prepared
cuz its gonna be a war
some kinda war
right here in the good old u/s/a
maybe not today but then again
what was that shit went down in philly
no good goode droppin bombs on black babies
and maybe you ain't like them rastas
or back ta africas or
whatever else the motherfuckas call themselves
cuz yea i know/niggas is not clean
i done smelled they stinkin ass hair
clumps a dirt and shit
smell like some motherfuckin camels
come on already
droppin bombs on little black babies
and of course some nigga had ta give the order
droppin bombs from a helicopter
on top a house full a little black babies
now how a brother gonna do that
cuz the motherfuckas run shit told him to

no it ain't no politicians
it's them five percenters
not the offshoot muslim thing
the five percent of the motherfuckas
that owns eighty-five percent of the loot
see
they pay the politicians
then the politicians got ta do what they say
and the police work for the politicians
and that no good goode was the police chief
so of course he though he was the man
but he wasn't no man cuz they said
"kill them pygmys...
or we'll fuck your momma in her black ass..."
and thats how they got that no good nigga
ta bomb a house full a little black babies
then he tried ta explain but couldn't say shit
killed eleven motherfuckas
and burnt down like sixty-two townhouses
then the stupid niggas who was complainin
complainin bout the kids
the kids runnin round naked
yea all naked and shit
shittin on they lawn but shit
thats they lawn
besides
they use shit as fertilizer anyway
thats why them rastas lawn was so green
and they weed be so mean i mean
they coulda used fertilizer ta make a bomb
like the whiteboys do
but i don't see them killin no whiteboys
motherfuck waco cuz see
it was a nigga up in there
and the feds was really after his black ass

open season

innocent victims slaughtered
and we dare protest the act
when in fact
it gets worse

a young girl shot
protecting fur
which
never really
belonged to her
how ironic and so
very sick

murdered for something
already killed
now the
media's thrilled
another death
makes no sense there
is no defense
for helpless creatures
or
unsuspecting children
of crimes
so similar

yet the children
warrant
no protest

there are no cries of...
stop killing for coats
no boycotts of gunshops
while we lounge at home
hands on remotes
flipping channels

searching for news
never feeling
their blues because
it has not happened
to us

we are insulated
like sheep with wool
kept warm
from bitter cold
and what makes a person
so bold
to demand the coat
from another's back
it's compassion they lack
we can't
blame this on crack
the problem runs
much deeper than that

it would seem
self esteem
could prevent
such a heinous crime
yet it happens
all the time
and
no one is innocent
we all own
leather and suede
and are now afraid
to wear it

and it's freezing outside
while inside we must hide
fearful of
losing our lives
over pieces of skin

so violently stripped
from it's original owner

and they die
to satisfy
the want and need of
greed and grand
slamming the door of compassion
on our children
these slaves
to fur and fashion

— margaret hague

urban haiku

homeboy i feels worse
then yo momma on the first
check is late again

blood on the keys

tranes a comin
and im a hummin
cuz eyes hurtin real bad
but
what else is new
kinda blue
no burnt describes it better
but diz said it best
nappy as a nite in tunisia
couldn't even please her once
but
tranes a comin
crusin on down the track
trip/switched
through a lite haze
heaven cant be but a
double-dutch skip jump away
and i wonder
when
where
why cant i share this
gretchen like grief
with someone other than my
micro-mini
stereo...stereo...stereo
stylistics kickin love ballistics
twistin my
heartaches like earthquakes
in a southern cali beachfront town
so damn down ups way below
sea level see
love dont love nobody
lessin its
a love supreme
not the bein but the feelin
cuz thats my god

hard grey-slate taste
which roams in my mouth
when i aint spoken to
another pair of eyes in daze
trane plays while my baby
lays me down at dawn
gone like every woman
since the birth
of my mothers death
requesting happiness is a
hollow hurt
haunting my every waking desire
didnt i blow your mind this time
it would end and begin
at the same moment
not on the outside but inside
where wrong is that
which frightens me most
more than moms ghost playin
guess how many jellybeans r
black & broken
and he was only jokin when he screamed
"yo momma"
"his moms is dead
and I'll kick all you'll niggas ass
if that shits said again!"
then
i couldnt hang
had ta hold my tyrant tongue
air lungs in otherways
created a
creature of habit
this heroin robot
controlled by the fear of
thinking alone
i'd become a
full grown home blown emotional parapalegic
in search of foreign lesions

within the wine bottled confines of
lafayette park
awash in the shadow of this
rustic slut
decked in decadence
fenced by a force so foul yet invisible
it resented its own
make-shift shallow reflection
introspective
indigestive
pseudo-noveau diet
kinda like a sly stone quiet riot
right-just/rebellious/religous beliefs
but they was always laffin
at my front teeth
bucks like the dollar two
crazy-glue couldnt keep us together
she
the better half of a whole wheat note
ms. mammy wrote sayin i was sick
but i was just sad my moms passed
"put that broom down
you aint clean shit
while she was around"
brown sugar melted
oatmeal lumped
bumped my head
falling from the back of a
speeding truck
lucky i aint die
humungus knott plus
two blue-black eyes for my
trouble...trouble...trouble...
bubblegum stuck to the end of a stick
nit pickin fishin for coins
corrupted/conceited
nick-named special ed.
shared a spring with three

but my pops moms
had the nerve to call it a bed
head had holes
when i woke
told to shush
before i spoke
which caused tears to roll
like roaches
crawlin up the wall
in a room with no door
we wasnt poor sure
I wore bernie beckles clothes
but everybody knows it wuz cuz
his moms wuz madd nice
franco american chicken gravy and rice
for breakfast
baloney and butter on wonder
for lunch
for dinner
pot lucky if anything was in the pot
but i got over it
made it on through cuz
kinda blue
soothed my soul
satinized my sAtanized ears
punk my years groovin ta
africa brass
a shape of jazz to come
had some sorta reason
to be be beleivin
be alright
gonna be alright
everything is gonna be alright
and now at nite
though i see blood/stained keys
dancin in my head
no more spring
bed now called futon

and ive gone way beyond
my most morbid expectations
trippin travlin tastin
bits a culture
i'd never knew
still
skeezin with bird
scattin with billie
rarely feelin kinda
blue is the lite
which illuminates the darkest steps
which lead to my dogwar dawns
lite like my moms words when she said
son
every goodbye
aint gone ...

steppo's attic

and i knows we wuz wrong for givin her static
so steppo and me went up to the attic to get high
why you have to go and die step
wasn't bout no rep but bout our pops not bein round
fudge brown rocks would set things right though
warm my jones cleanse my soul so the pain would subside
ridin the witch
what brother earl would say but
he ain't know it hurt so bad ta be so mad every god/damn day
least that nigga had a moms who
hugged him kissed him even missed him
when we played hookey from school so
scag became my mother
when i discovered what it meant to be in a
six feet knee deep hell like hole
noddin with god/when some olive oil greaseball said
"sell it to the coloreds...let them lose their souls!"
and that shit slapped the slop that was slippin from my lip
ceased scratchin my dick and attempted to figure if shit was real
see/what you feel and how you think cuz
many a fetus been flushed down the sink though bev bore ten
when I can't send love letters much less
remember shit by heart there's no heat my head hurts
it's not her i blame for this game a cat and mouse
I been losin for life
love the one you're with
shit...
I hate everybody but me and don't love myself
a wealth a talent gone to waste chasin a taste
watchin the ghost of xmas past burn yulelogs
while we booted twice
nice neat piles would last awhile we nodded and farted
and fucked with each other's head
psycho-ghetto therapy cost less than the couch
plus i ain't have to hear that bitches motherfuckin mouth
askin if my pops beat my moms with his blackjack or his belt

but that shit felt good...
had me strokin my wood scratchin my nose
bendin over backwards tryin to kiss my toes
but a nigga knows when shit ain't right
turned to lite a square and right there
stretched on the floor was step
nigga o/deed
and i'm noddin and sobbin while thinkin
i'm a need me a new dopefiend friend then
some other shit went down...

first time

steps swept round
you
at the bottom stood
lookin good
skin brown
as bright light leaked
from some
cheap yellow bulb
bout ta bend
bout ta be
bout ta see what this
"s" thing was
all about
lips pressed
couldn't shout
cuz if grandma heard
she'd be
whippin whippin whippin
your ass
wanted ta go
oh so slow
but ya
know know know
fast ain't half bad

madd nasty
stairway gettin funky
never figured
it would taste like this
first kiss
first time
grindin up against a
curve in the wall
tryin desperately not ta fall
fingers fumblin
mumblin somethin bout love

lappin
lustin
bustin slob
turnin knobs
we ain't even know we had
scared
embarassed but
damn glad

sweat dripped down
tongues slid round like
glint eyed lizards
lickin low green grass
time flew
fast don't do justice
maybe quick like toast
already thinkin bout
boastin bout
what we'd done
big fun
felt funny
on the money
i think

gave me a drink of
warm red wine
found lost time
feelin/fraid but proud
was we loud
did anybody hear
held you near
stroked your
coarse kinky hair
as we fell aimlessly
to the bottom step
of the
dimly lit
curved stair

caring glaring eyes
paint brushing
bewitching brown thighs
with my index
finger
finger
finger...

moments lingered
time ta go
stood slowly
like my
great great grandfather
whose crook-legged image loomed
larger than life
larger than breaths faked
alley cat scratchin voice cryin out
"son
don't be makin no mistakes!"
but those
languid lakes
which silently sat
behind your still/life eyes
let me know the choice we made
was definitey wise...

149th and 3rd

but it didn't last long
cuz she couldn't stand the lies
my ego's size
or the gettin high but...

looking back
i see pitch black confusion
illusions of poverty pain
the number two train
flailing wailing
uptown Bronx bound
donde boricua
been downtown selling
coca y estofa
para miha y miho
"adios mios"
mamita screams
but hey i got dreams
and it seems like
ice cream cones and
dopefiend jones
go hand in hand
and the man is the mack
while jack told jill
she better pop that pill
or he will hang her out to dry
she cries
eyelids droop
from shootin hops
too dumb to drop this
quick/cop habit
shit can't quit
as mamita lit vente uno candles
can't handle no more
poor baby
maybe she came off too

mucho mas fria
kneeling to santeria
ow mama mia
what a big a/zoo/pep
strep throat junkies gloat
it's time for
wine women swimmin in cerveza
"mira mommi
lookin good baby
fuck you bitch
e/su/see/ah..."
la la la la la la
tito puenete say baile
timbales booming
lebron brothers crooning
"i'm so tired/i do the boogaloo"
what you think
we didn't knew you was puertoriqueno
so what the fuck is up bro
like in
mucho dinero
you get para
mucho trabajo
coppin blow on 152nd & Jackson
where's there's action 24-7
and heaven is speedballs
shot in piss/stained halls
donde esta la heat
and the meat you beat
ain't lechon cabron
domun baso de leche
"pepe it's mamita day"
play numero uno uno cuatro
go low so low you ho
puta/bruja
your mama not mine
slime slam slim is
"loose joints"

as policia points tech nine
what time is it
que hora es
mess with me
you gonna see jesus
riding the back of
suavacita's caboose
loose loud well endowed
proud of her three bambinos
and three bedroom section eight
waiting on food stamps
while junkies camp out under
dim/wit lit streets
pumas on feet
checkin out the
sweet pleated girl from jersey
with the jumbo juicy pussy
blushing beaming rosa red
soon to be in wolfy's bed
head bangin wall
wolfy braggin ten feet tall
after dropping his load
he shoots to the mall
and the
juicy lucy lazy latina
sips tequila at cantina
suckin down a new high in lows and
nobody knows
the trouble she's seen
clean mean spleen blown away
cuz she wouldn't say "sorry"
for steppin on the
confused crews shoes
losers winners sinners suckers
dumb luck schmucks
blind bucks living for machismo
as a tree grows on neon sidewalks
muggers stalk helpless prey

a day in may
a.k.a.
cinco de mayo
"me no cholo
me no mexicano
me puerto rican!"
would you mind repeating that again
gracias martita morales para
"¿mami...mami...mami...
por que tu blanca y papi tan"
mixed races empty faces car chases and
da/da/da da da
car jacks
plus vials of crack equals
bullet riddled brains the norm
storms brew
black cows moo
shoes fly
wiseguys stuff pasta
while rastas take control of the
once upon a time in america
i want to pee on america
huh
what you say
jose cuervo
"yo mang who's gots da blow?"
a snow storm of enormous proportions
along side blackdoor abortions
consorted contortions concealed
give the sign to steal
no
not second base
that case of champale
now poppi's in jail
going mucho insane
so much pain
so much pain
no mas pain

cocaine
y cocoa bread
fed a stedy diet of
rice & beans
phony green card
repeat offender retards
guarding el barrio
as miho y miha
fill the tips of their
almost golden noses
praying to moses
playing the fool
so cool
so cool
so cool
is kool-aid
elephant piss green gatorade
and ten cans of raid
to kill
"la cucaracha
la cucaracha
mira!"
it's the wizard of oz
no
it's only tony
remember
he use to be a he
but now he is a she
and ain't
nada para free
not
pussy/dew/gee/poverty or death
the only question is...

por que tu padre

por que tu padre
grab his machete
when he caught us kissin
on the kitchen floor
god/damn moreno
he screamed
as the street lite beamed
from the gleaming blade

scared shitless
bout ta break
wished so
wanted to
take you yet knew
the love of my life was
my love of this life
besides
the sound of that
sharp ass knife
clanging against the
heatless pipe
left little time ta think

brushed beside the broken bannister
just beyond reach
he screachin
she cryin
feet flyin to the bottom
ready to bolt
but first had to unbolt
then manuever a maze of
semi-exotic locks

once out got my
second wind blowin
like louisiana lightnin throwin

toein ground
headed for the
two bucks in pocket
roarin like a rocket
rose like edwin moses
in a gold medal
leaped up and over
the broken turnstile
while waiting waiting waiting
I'm brewin brewin brewin
just hating the
hating the
greasy-headed jibaro
then i noticed
snowflakes fallin
and somebody
callin my name

hawk came whining
like the
wicked witch of the west
over top a
high-rise shack
#2 cruisin through
on the
wrong damn track
and like the snow
i'm driftin back
to the nite
i met maria

it was a
b/ball game
hoboken rec
no sweat
bust they ass
cuz we played fast
both on and off

tackheads from teenpost
thought most hadn't seen
teens in years

few beers
some cheeb
lil sniff
ta set us straight
couldn't wait ta run
with the big time guns
from lafayette
backed by a bunch a bookies
always makin wild bets

but we had hoop legends
who forever be forgettin
they age and they names
bad ass niggas
with too much game
shame some a the shit
happened to them
as for me
I just wanted to win

lay-up line
time to freak for the folks
from frank's hometown
and man
did we throw down
three-sixties
double-pumps
shakin rumps
breakin rims
and then she walked in
"mira
que linda
presiosa
mami"

i swiveled and stared
she was lookin at me

now bein a super highway
mellow kinda yellow
thoroughly disgusted
and forever mistaken
for a kinky-headed Puerto Rican
but maria's almond joy eyes
had me mesmerized
and feelin kinda new

du/tap tip his hat
as she started smilin
real sweet like
right then and there
i knew we'd be tight

that nite
was on top my game
drove them niggas insane
with my
dapper dan handle
and
hiroshima hop
couldn't be
wouldn't be
niggas wished they could
stop me
kicked mucho booty
won mvp
let maria hold the trophy

suddenly
shadows turned to sound
maria's pops
blade in hand
came flyin up the steps

steam streamin from his
bull shaped nose

frozen toes awoke
as i broke down the platform
wind blowin/snow flailin
and here comes the 2
sailin up the track
jumps in on time
swearin ta god
i ain't never comin back
to 152nd and jackson ave

if she's darker than your sister (we don't need her in this house)

the blacker the berry
the blacker the berry
the blacker the berry
the tighter the noose
wrapped round my neck
put in check by my
suspect grandmother
who
despite being
spiteful/deceitful/constipated
and caught up in an
assimilated assumption
was still my best friend

schooled in the virtues of
theater
art
the evils of headstart
stereotyped and steeped
in the
light/skinned syndrome
"don't bring that black nigger home!"
she repeatedly screamed
while poignantly pouring heavy cream
into my midnite cappucino

afros was out
can still hear shouts of
"you look like watusis"
excuse me please
i thought that we's was black
but in fact she thought
nothing of the sort
so i
aborted my distorted

tragic mullatto mission
and began fishin
for a girlfriend
ten tones darker than me
this brought grandma
mucho misery
excedrin headaches #1 through 99
and no matter how fine my friend
the end would begin
at the end of a noose
she'd only loosen up
when i began to date the daughter of a
prototype bup "easy...

i'm sure penelope
is not use
to all this ruff/housing"
bring me the
bring me the
bring me the
bring me the
"bring me the picture of dorothy dandridge"
who?
"the one on my nightstand
and hand me my pack of frappe"
which i thought until recently
was just a cool way to say
cigarette in french

"my dear...
you're far more pretty than that
dark/skinned winch my heathen grandson
use to date"
needless to say i
hated myself
hated her too
never knew why i'd cry
whenever that fat black maid

came in from the rain
to fetch her white/like kid
she hid then denied
i cried then lied about
who i was
from wince i came
ashamed beyond belief but
at grandmother's wake
all concerned
were shocked i showed no grief
expressing motionless emotion

for you see there would be
no more
perfumed lotion
spear/chucked remarks
no more harks from herald angels
routinely dangled from
freshly chopped pine
no more blackeye peas
and no more god/damn motherfuckin swine

just time to forget
time to move on
to the heat of my nite
not the break of her dawn
to get deep down and dirty
to get back to my roots but
gots ta be careful
wouldn't want to soil my
brand new three-piece
brooks brother suit

everybody

everybody wants to help you out
everybody wants to be your friend
everybody wants to free the fright
at the end of the
funnel/funnel/funnel...
everybody wants to be or not to be
left out in the cold
everybody wants to act like they told you so
when you ain't heard shit
everybody wants to be everything
swinging tight-lipped-lust
when its love you need
everybody wants to
nick you
cut you
slice you
til you bleed to death
everybody thinks they're the best
but once you put your money
where your mouth use to be
then all the sudden
everybody wants to be like you
everybody til somebody new comes along
dancin/prancin and romancin the crowd
somebody loud and obnoxious
somebody with a bigger
click-clack-clankin right on by
somebody who can
lie/cheat/steal
somebody coppin a feel real slick like
somebody flyin the highest kite
somebody kissin you goodnite
like you ain't
never/ever/ever
been kissed before
somebody sure feels good

somebody would but won't last
somebody suckin up fast
with a sly ass grin
but when
somebody passes you by
don't look back
cuz you might like what you won't
see everybodys the same
not somebody
i said everybody
yea
everybodys the same
but me

trane takes 5

i like music more than books
not all kinds
mostly jazz
i remember two albums
well not the whole albums
but two songs from two albums
that was my favorite songs
yea
was my favorite things
trane
daddy called him trane
and at first i thought
nigga was the brother
be collectin tickets
on the amtrak to newark
we had relatives in newark
i think thats the first time
i ever seen them nation of islam niggas
but i soon found out
his name was trane
coltrane
he was my favorite
i mean that song was my favorite
my favorite things made me happy
happy like i ain't never felt before
or since
but the funny thing was
whenever i heard that shit
i felt happy
but it made me cry
i don't know why
i would run into my room
hide my face in the pillow
be cryin like crazy
and i remember my favorite things got me a "d"
thats right

a "d" in english
sixth grade
it was miss delaney in sixth grade
we went on this field trip
why they call it a field trip
we never went to no field
nor seen no grass or no trees
was always some silly museums
like edisons lighthouse
which made no damn sense
cuz the shit was dark
or the movies
miss delaney was good for the movies
i think she like dark places
cuz she was an ugly motherfucka
but i got a "d" in english
english composition
cuz we was sposed to write a composition
bout some stupid movie
it was the sound of music
but the shit ain't sound like no music to me
sounded like turkeys screamin
bout to get their heads handed to em
yea it was bullshit
except for one song
cuz to be honest i fell asleep
i wasn't gonna pass anyway cuz i fell asleep
only reason i seen any of it
cuz i heard this song
sounded like something i knew
but i couldn't place it
then it hit me
it was trane/thats right/coltrane
my favorite song
my favorite things
and this chicken neck lady
daddy had to be a butcher
cuz thats what she did to tranes song

i mean i wish i had a brick
cuz i'd a thrown it right threw the screen
so we gotta write a composition bout the movie
and i wrote how disgraceful it was
that this chicken neck lady butchered tranes song
i shoulda got a "a"
cuz in composition it's all about description
i described that bitch to a tee
she all homely and shit
wearin them old raggedy long ass clothes
look like the same shit grandma mcduff wear
when she go clean them rich whitefolks homes
and her hair
look just like a boy
so when the man kiss her i'm thinkin
they must be faggots or somethin
cuz she sure look like a man to me
so i got a "d" but fuck miss delaney
she look like a boy too
you know
now that i think about it
her and miss close use to sit awfully close
sippin out each others coke
sharin popcorn too
i shoulda knew
but i was only in the sixth grade

now the other album never made me cry
it was by some white guy
only white guy my daddy liked
and he would listen to the song
like damn near hundred times in a row
it always made him fall asleep
made me wanna snap my fingers
but he be sleep
not snorin though
his head be swayin back and forth
and he be scratchin his nutsack

and sometimes no most times
he be smokin a cigarrette
til it burn right down to the end
couple times it burnt his fingers
but he ain't even feel it
i had to wipe his mouth once
cuz slob was runnin all down his chin
take five never did that to me
so i'm watchin t.v. and i hear it
then i sees this crazy lookin whiteman
craziest lookin whiteman i ever seen
and he talkin bout some car called infiniti
and i hear that song
and it sound so good
make me start payin attention
to what he was sayin bout the car
well he really wasn't talkin bout the car
he was sayin some shit bout
why did i do this
and i'm thinkin hey
i ain't do shit
then my head starts swayin back and forth
and i'm scratchin and noddin and slobbin
but i could still hear this crazy man
my eyes were closed but i was wide awake
all i could think about was that car
that infiniti
and i love that music and the words too
sounded like a poem
and it came on every ten minutes
so after awhile i could say it
so then i sit down and start to write
but it wasn't a poem
it was a commercial for t.v.
commercial bout that infiniti
cept it was niggas ridin in the car
ridin down 135th right near strivers row
and they was dressed fine and cruisin slow

so all the other niggas
who was standin on the corners
could see they had this new infiniti
they was slappin each other five
cuz they was proud but then
some white people start honkin
honkin they horns
white people in hondas honkin in harlem
must a been comin from yankee stadium
cuz when it be a bunch a traffic
some stupid white people
try and take a shortcut through harlem
tryin to get back to saddle river or whatever
and they was honkin
tryin to make the niggas in the infiniti
speed the fuck up
started callin em coons and spearchuckers
then all the sudden
they crashed into each other
then the niggas who was hangin on the corners
climbed up into the whitefolks cars
and stole they shit
then here come the two niggas
cruisin in they infiniti
laffin they black asses off

so i loves music
not all kinds
just my favorite things
but you know another thing make me sick
is these niggas
these niggas on these talk shows
and even though they may look like us
they ain't really us but they
talk and talk and talk and talk and...

chase/n e.k.

sick a walkin
tired of talkin to tired clerks
tellin me they ain't got
what i want
needs to find some
black arts rhyme
done chased e.k. all day
see aloud sittin on the shelf
and one healthy presiosa
violatin ai
while cooling with baudelaire and bly
be beatty
his joker deuced
spruce goose collection of
rhythm and rhyme
a metaphorical metronome
verbally muggin time (from joker/joker deuce)
while just below
but slightly behind cries bryant
snuggled between
browning and burroughs
tight like dominican girdles (from song of the sirens)
laced round her
hip/jazzy class like toomer
less tame
but i still don't see names like
benson/medina/perdomo
guess folks don't know
who's droppin bombs
and i thought that was
the american dream
not the one sapphire be writin
bout to jump off the page
and eat your dick
and i'm sick a seein the
real world poets hair

blurbed by holman
oh no motherfucka
don't you dare
i stare at the cover of negrophobia
somehow sittin next to joyce
and i can almost hear darius' voice
"it do feel like a brillo pad" (from negrophobia)
mad ms. phenomenal
got a shelf to herself
while baraka ain't got but a book
called conversations
so why you'll don't talk to him
face to face to
pissed i almost missed
the mini/renaissance
cullen/hurston
langston hughes weary blues
flyin higher
than that tired ass dove
while just below
but depths above is
gerard manley hopkins
dead hundreds of years
pero...donde esta
pinero y esteves y dumas
and dunbar and walker
and jordan and harper
francis/not mike
patricia smith
nayo
and where the fuck is etheridge knight
out of print
this meant i had to go to newark
to search for the book
jumped on the path and realized
it's the first damn place
i should a looked

high page silence

the mud green bench
hard as pine
plays feathered bed
to chalk white skin
a straw haired head
chasing z's

pot filled breeze sweeps
sunlite peeps
through solemn trees
glazed glint hints of
beauty past
fast fading
this masquerading lady
known
as bag

magnified tear
from swollen eye
plops then sighs
obese belly
vanilla jelly
overlaps then nestles
upon tattered coat

overhead
clouds billow
below
trash serves as pillow
aluminum goldmine
sign of times

fire red alarm clocks screech
beseeching one who sleeps
to rise

head turns
cornflake fingers
burrow olive/drab enclave
eyes remain shut

but grey/brown nuts
and day old crumbs
cause frantic squirrels to pray
oblivious to
snores
coughs
emanating from breathing statue
who chooses
then snoozes
this scene

on the mud green bench
behind the iron wrought fence
beyond the towering arch
on this
lovely sunday morning
in washington square park

welcome to mcdonalds
(may i take your order please)

so i bust into mcdonalds and this sister ringing fries
is squabblin with this brother moppin the filthy floor
now the sister (who's kinda cute)
is in the process of bein steam/roomed by some buppy
who's droppin lines he must a lifted from some
nineteen seventies black exploitation flick
so the sisters pissed the brothers stressed
and the buppies new nikes was gettin wet
all this time i'm standin in line
tryin ta order a fish filet with no tartar
seems the sisters sick a ringing fries
cuz she hikes her hands rolls her eyes and says
"punk motherfucka coward ass bitch
your hairs too straight and you walk with a switch"
the buppies french wave stood at attention
as his boys frick and frack cracked the fuck up
then/the manager
who happened to be a male member of the
caucasian persuasion
tried ta pull a newt gingrich impersonation
and set the sister straight
so she hits void
snatches the cheese stained apron
from round her dancehall hips
pokes out her lip
then precedes to rip into the boss
who makes like forest gump
then runs to the back
and hides behind a freezer
meanwhile the brother with the mop
is diggin into his thick grey sock
tryin ta find a vial a rocks
seems like he got this slick lil hustle goin down
and like a circle is round we wind up back at me see
i was just tryin ta order a fish filet with no tartar

when i started gettin impatient
cuz you know how shit go at mickey dees
"when you gettin off?"
"girl how much your earings cost?"
"i heard she's fuckin the boss!"
and i shoulda been more patient
but i had to catch a bus
and maybe i need to get in touch
with my more sensitive side
but then i thought
fuck this shit
walked outside and split

hoetry haiku
(ripped off from tree)

if you can get paid
for some silly shit you made
best take the dough/hoe

ALSO FROM LONG SHOT:

I HAVE NO CLUE

Poems by

Jack Wiler

When I read the inimitable Jack Wiler, I can't tell if I'm laughing or crying, or being punched in the teeth by the Zeitgeist. Here is true grit, true rage, true fear and lust, true language. If you hate your job, read this book. Read it anyway. Face it and laugh.
—Alicia Ostriker

In Jack Wiler's world it's always busy for no discernible reason except so you can tell the difference between the working stiff and the stiff stiff. Wiler's the Poet of Scabs and Warts, where every glimmer has a slammer, a can of can't, a dose of don't. This is where dogs bang into fences, the purpose of a lover is to walk out on you, where beer goes flat as it hits the air. But the rats sit there in the Catchmaster Rat Glueboards staring you down, daring you to write a poem, write that sucker down. There's only one poet on earth who dares write this one. Hooray for Jack Wiler, Messenger of the Gods.
—Bob Holman

good poetry works. good poets work til it hurts. jack wiler makes us hurt and work and hurt some more. his poems arch their backs bellowing echoes which push us closer to crystal silence. it's time to go to work.
—reg e gaines

Order your copy by sending $7.95 to
(NJ residents add 47¢ sales tax)
Long Shot Productions
PO Box 6238
Hoboken, NJ 07030

101 Reasons to Read Long Shot

Miguel Algarin, Antler, Ida Applebroog, Amina Baraka, Amiri Baraka, Hugo Bastidas, Paul Beatty, Wallace Berman, Ted Berrigan, Joseph Beuys, Jennifer Blowdryer, Ray Bremser, Charles Bukowski, William Burroughs, Janet Cannon, Steve Cannon, Jim Carroll, Noam Chomsky, Cheryl Clark, Larry Clark, Andy Clausen, John Coltrane, Sue Coe, Gregory Corso, Jayne Cortez, Victor Hernandez Cruz, Disposable Heroes of Hiphoprisy, Tim Dlugos, Sharon Doubiago, Eric Drooker, Charles Dumas, Martin Espada, Maggie Estep, Lawrence Ferlinghetti, Reg E. Gaines, Allen Ginsberg, Leon Golub, Richard Hell, Eva Hesse, Abbie Hoffman, Jack Hirschman, Bob Holman, Lorri Jackson, Ted Joans, Hettie Jones, June Jordan, Eliot Katz, Yitzhak Katzenelson, Komar & Melamid, Tuli Kupferberg, Jack Kerouac, Latin Empire, June Leaf, Thomas Lux, Nancy Mercado, Bobby Miller, Elizabeth Murray, Eileen Myles, Cookie Mueller, Jack Micheline, Alice Notley, Ric Ocasek, Yoko Ono, Peter Orlovsky, Alicia Ostriker, Pedro Pietri, Sean Penn, Stuart Z. Perkoff, Marge Piercy, Robert Press, Leaping Lanny Poffo, Ishmael Reed, Lou Reed, Adrienne Rich, Larry Rivers, Luis J. Rodriguez, Sonia Sanchez, Ed Sanders, George Segal, Mary Shanley, Cindy Sherman, Danny Shot, Hersch Silverman, Nancy Spero, Lamont Steptoe, Piri Thomas, Susie Timmons, Edwin Torres, Quincy Troupe, Janine Pommy Vega, Julia Vinograd, Anne Waldman, Diane Wakoski, Tom Waits, Jack Wiler, Danielle Willis, George C. Wolfe, Phil Zwickler

☐ **Subscribe to Long Shot for the next two years (four issue) for only $24.00**

Writing for the Real World!!!

Make checks payable to:

**Long Shot Productions
P.O. Box 6238
Hoboken, NJ 07030**